THE FAR MOSQUE

Also by Kazim Ali

Quinn's Passage: A Novel

The Far Mosque

Kazim Ali

Alice James Books

FARMINGTON, MAINE

10 9 8 7 6 5 4 3 2 1

Alice James Books are published by Alice James Poetry Cooperative, Inc.,
an affiliate of the University of Maine at Farmington.

ALICE JAMES BOOKS
238 MAIN STREET
FARMINGTON, ME 04938

www.alicejamesbooks.org

Library of Congress Cataloging-in-Publication Data
Ali, Kazim, 1971–
The far mosque / Kazim Ali.
   p.   cm.
ISBN–13: 978–1–882295–53–1
ISBN–10: 1–882295–53–6 (pbk.)
I. Title.

PS3601.L375F37 2005
811'.6—dc22   2005009740

Alice James Book gratefully acknowledges support from the University of Maine
at Farmington and the National Endowment for the Arts. 🌱

COVER: Detail of "Mosque" by Kazim Ali
INTERIOR: Geometric Pattern by Marco Wilkinson

CONTENTS

🐚 I

🐚 2

ACKNOWLEDGMENTS

I am grateful to the editors of the journals and periodicals *Americn Poet, Beacon Dispatch, Catamaran, Colorado Review, Five Fingers Review, Hayden's Ferry Review, The Iowa Review, Mirage #4/Period(ical), Rattapallax, Second Avenue Poetry, Sentence: a Journal of Prose Poetics, Washington Square* and *Xcp (Cross-Cultural Poetics)*, and the anthologies *Risen From the East* and *Writing the Lines of Our Hands*, where many of these poems appeared in earlier versions.

Thank you to Jennifer Chapis, Hyder Aga, Jean Valentine, Sean Safford, Kavitha Rao and Jeff Golden. To my teachers and fellow students in the NYU Creative Writing Program. To Kathy Graber who assembled the earliest version of this book from a folder of loose poems. To Agha Shahid Ali. And deeply, to Zehra Begum, to the entire extended Ali/Saeed family and to Marco Wilkinson.

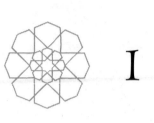

I

Gallery

You came to the desert, illiterate, spirit-ridden,
intending to starve

The sun hand of the violin carving through space
the endless landscape

Acres of ochre, the dust-blue sky,
or the strange young man beside you

peering into "The Man Who Taught William Blake
Painting in His Dreams"

You're thinking: *I am ready to be touched now, ready to be found*
He's thinking: *How lost, how endless I feel this afternoon*

When will you know:
all night: sounds

Violet's brief engines
The violin's empty stomach resonates

Music a scar unraveling in four strings
An army of hungry notes shiver down

You came to the desert intending to starve   so starve

Renunciation

"The Sailor cannot see the North—but knows the Needle can—"

The books were all torn apart, sliced along the spines
Light filled all the openings that she in her silence renounced

Still: her handwriting on the papers remembered us to her
The careful matching of the papers' edges was a road back

One night Muhummad was borne aloft by a winged horse
Taken from the Near Mosque to the Far Mosque

Each book likens itself to lichen,
stitching softly to tree trunks, to rocks

what was given into the Prophet's ears that night:
A changing of directions—now all the scattered tribes must pray:

Wonder well foundry, well sunborn, sundered and sound here
Well you be found here, foundered and found

The Agnes Martin Room

What is a question to someone who practices years of silence?

Stones skim the water's surface, shimmer there, lost.

In the window sound of last year.

Swim dimmer there.

After four days without speaking, I don't ask questions anymore.

Given a line, draw through space.

Reach to reason to region.   To seem or sum
Sun or stone.

Could weep here.

Sleep here.

In the sweep of watery gray.

On white, the wishes, the whispered accounts,
a little autobiography, littered on the surface.

Where we listen. Were we here.

Unaccountable dark matter of the universe,
an utterly supportless planet. Ocean of space.

All the same river to read. All shapes or landscape.

The scapegoat silent, following the road of devotion.

Going down without air.

Sounds like the rope against the side of the boat, a hollow bell.

Get subtler and subtler in the acres of water until
one refuses to return.

Spirit send the question sound.

Painting is the quicksand back.

Two tracks over the seeming field of white.

All the eventual answers are nothing.

Painting is asking you.

No time is passing.

The River Cloud

On paper, on the sky, on the river's mad meniscus

I've drawn a blank

Remaindered against the banks, pressed there by the current

The river dispersing into the light gray

Cloud me down by the river edged with willow

The smoke of the river cloud canticles

A thought river between shores leads out and out

River draw all this through me

What's hidden beneath the hull of the boat

Or in the cloud of the river

Future river feeding

The charts are no good

The far shore disappears

Give it to me now to live

In the river's unmaking epoch

Locking itself into the oars

Onto the boat my cloud

Boat my body

Body my oar

Oar and fog

Fog oar rowing

Cloud oar rowing

Prayer

Four green threads interrogate the wind.
Pilgrims tie them to the iron fence around the saint's tomb.

Each thread is a prayer. Each prayer is a chance to weave.
I do not want to return home without that which I came for.

The poet was here—but he's gone now—
you've missed him.

The river turns three times on the journey home.
I have to tie the thread around my own wrist bone.

One Evening

(a version of Iqbal)

The half-light of the moon is silent.
Every tree's branches are silent.

The morning songs of the bright birds do not linger.
The hillside, swathed in green, sleeps.

Even the river slows. The church bells do not echo.
Silence stretches low over the valley.

My heart, you too should try silence.
Invite this sadness in to sleep.

Night

Up against the window, the fading sun.
In rags, Orion's notes appear against your skin.

Sparsely thrown across your chest.
Swathed in the folds of blankets.

Now you are luminous.
The bow no longer exists.

The star chart I traced into the palm of my hand.
Has smoke written all through it.

Are you terrified of absolute silence?
I drive miles into the country just to have a look at you.

You are no plagiarist of dusk.
Nothing in the sky equals itself.

All the stars have changed positions.
All the fortunes have been faked.

Charted against a lover who hasn't existed for a million years.

Source

In the brain, a silver window
Where the sky evaporates—

Then condenses to an enveloped name
Sealed with an unsigned letter.

Dickinson's house: a breeze coming from the inside
Sounds bury themselves deep in the woodwork.

When a Scholar pauses by a closed door
She may not be listening to the music, but to the door

What lingers in the letter, loosening or found
Sky-name—wood-wind—syllable—sound

Speech

How struck I was by that face, years ago, in the church mural:
Eve, being led by Christ through the broken gates of Hell.

She's been nominated for the position of Featured Saint
on the Icon of Belief, up against the dark horse candidate—

me: fever-ridden and delirious, a child in Vellore, unfolding
the packet around my neck that I was ordered not to open.

Inside, a folk cure, painted delicately in saffron.
Letters that I could not read.

Why I feel qualified for the position
based on letters I could not read amounts to this:

Neither you nor I can pronounce the difference
between the broken gates and the forbidden letters.

So what reason do we need to believe in icons or saints?
How might we otherwise remember—

without an image to fasten in that lonely place—
the rock on which a Prophet flung himself into fever?

Without icon or church, spell "gates of Hell."
Spell "those years ago unfolding."

Recite to me please all the letters you are not able to read.
Spell "fling yourself skyward."

Spell "fever."

Agnes Martin

Wetten to work here seen against the sky sandscape sandbox silent

Alone mind unleashed mouth a close open cave stone breathe

Stone whiten away sharp sky edge dusk blend down dark self edge

Thrown aloft five birds little surface wind lettered and fettered

Distant sounds littered across thoughts sounds blanked pulled taut

Spun thunder then well spread encumbered better window bitter

Sun wind whispered winter went indigo wild wick lit wend home

Sleep-written swept sweetly remind here my mend here my mind

Hear sweep music slides fabric oceanic oh shine year light shine

Year come time ear tie signs and sing why think river open heart I

Cornflower cowslip field wind settled across year sound thrown

Settled to end hear whittled to wend—

Travel

Soon to leave

Soon across the water

Prepare the white clothes

I will not plan the painting

But travel—the trees—

Looking out over the roofs

Rather lay paint directly on the canvas

Kate writes from Paris, in smoke

I can't respond but pack

The painting is not finished until the original idea has been

Taken down from the walls

All the paintings

Enough nomad, move through "soon"

Move through

Obliterated

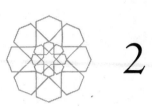

2

Night Boat

At some point in the calanques above Cassis
You were told by Mister Stevarius the Belgian Fire Eater

Fallen down the mountain the lights of the night boat to Corsica
Disappear the rock of Cassis, thrust out into the sea

That there would be a moment at which

The road to the temple of the sun threads its secret way
From the violent tongue of the third calanque to the rocky alcove

Where the cliff-climbers muscle their way up, unsupported

You would no longer hear

Everyone is talking loud
The schoolteacher from Aix is drunk

And the accountant from Switzerland
Calls the German a bastard for not sharing his coffee

There you are on the night boat, hungry
Fire on the surface of the water

Letters collecting in the groundswell
You will not hear

On the beach of sound, waves roam back to open sea
Close to the surface the sun's setting pools orange

An opening of light in the sky
A stripe of rubble you've never seen before

Unfurl your hands to say: *You will no longer here*
The trees are rapt with silence

The burning bird settling in the rocks
Stand ever among the broken vowels:

You will no longer hour

The silent groundswell, the swell of silence.

Train Ride

We take a compartment. I draw the curtains and shut the door so that other passengers will believe the seats are all filled and leave us.

This rudeness is against my cousin's instincts, so I let him take the backwards facing seat.

He says it is the proper way to view the landscape.

That night in Aix-en-Provence we won't be able to find a hotel, and the hostel will be closed.

We will spend all night in the public square, reciting poetry to one another, and receiving gifts from the late night locals.

Flowers, drawings, hot pastries.

This moment now gone.

I time everything to that current of lapse.

No absent time.

Even in deep space, there are particles of dark matter that do not add to the mass of the universe.

Versions of the story wither over sacred fire. A prophet's willingness to be blind.

We travel alone all the way to Marseille. Or: while my cousin uses the bathroom, two girls come to sit with me.

We have to switch trains at Dijon. Or: we never make it as far as Aix.

The source of a vision only a priestess getting high on fumes.

Snake-licked. Shucking off the old skin.

Blessed be the undone version. The train actually stalls on the tracks for several hours, during which we contemplate returning to Paris.

It might only be a condition of the window-glass that allows me to see the subtle ridges and gradations in the clouds, the swirling depth of the sky.

A Cézanne painting on the cover of *The World of the Ten Thousand Things* is so deathly unfinished it looks nearly transparent. Pencil marks on the canvas.

Later, in a vestibule between cars, the Provençal sun setting, I catch sight of the book's cover in the reflection of the window.

Flooded with bright orange and yellow the painting completes itself.

Is that all: a quest for fulfillment satisfied by the correct conditions? In this case, supposed chromatic equations of the southern skies—my cousin explains it: yellow in Arles, green in Aix, purple on the Côte d'Azur.

Later he will return to Paris, and I will hike alone to Ste-Maries-de-la-Mer where Magdalen supposedly washed ashore with her servant Sarah. Their bones are in a reliquary in the church.

Yet another church miles and miles to the north and east of here continues the story: Magdalen left her servant and traveled inland with the gypsies and died there.

Another set of bones in that church.

Unlike in mathematics, every quadratic equation in history does not necessarily have an equivalent modular form.

Small handfuls only create an impression of a manageable amount to hold. For example, I have left out the wild flamingos, a subtle swipe of pale pink along their pearl-white bodies, flying across the road; also the horse-back ride through the swamps of the Cammargue, the hours I sat in the small shack in the bird sanctuary, the black-clad gypsy woman I saw in the market.

In the gypsy fortune-telling book, past and future shuffle and re-shuffle.

As our journey progresses we do eventually open the curtains and the compartment fills.

We eat the previously unmentioned camembert sandwiches.

We won't arrive in Aix for several more hours and don't go on to Cassis for four more days after that.

Where, in another four days, in the mountains above the city, tired and out of money and ready to go home, we will meet Mister Stevarius, the Belgian Fire Eater, and everything changes.

The Studio

Great northern window and sheets of light.
Wine has evaporated in the glass, leaving a burgundy crust.

How shall I find you?

My travel case is packed and
sitting by the door

Rotted fruit. Skulls.
Paint marks on every table and chair.

How shall I find you?

My coat is hanging on the hook

My cane is leaning there

Who are you looking for

The Cemetery at Montparnasse

Each stone is speaking in tongues:
Mon travail est ma prière.

One of the dead is born in my birth year.

An open mausoleum, empty of urns.
Blue sky seen through the shattered window.

Near the gate Sartre and de Bouvoir buried in a single grave.

Scattered across their cenotaph an alphabet of stones,
dried flowers, museum tickets.

All prayers to our passing.

My stone-tongued mouth.

My work is my prayer.

Rouen

The cathedral ruined, smoke-charred, empty.
All the stained glass replaced by clear panes.

Somewhere in the garden, unmarked
among weeds and branches spiring skywards,

the grove where Jeanne was burned.

High above the floor in the spaces of the roof,
on a catwalk, a worker cleans the windows.

Somewhere in this cathedral dark stairs lead to that place.

Through the dark-blue window it's 1942:
the war has come to Rouen.

Ravens swoop down.
All the windows shatter.

Chunks of roof breaking off—falling—
The floor littered with prismatic rain.

The statue cracks to rubble on its pedestal.
The chapels on the south wall shudder.

One after the other collapse to dust.

The nave creaks and pitches, rising and keeling
atop the flood of light.

Every saint's image has disappeared save one:
Ste-Catherine being stretched on her wheel—

Her stone arms alone hold the long south wall.
Who is the brave one? Who has been called?

Harmony unbuckles as Jeanne turns her head to answer.
The long walk goes through shadow and arch to the garden grove.

The music is snapping, thread by thread.

The statues are all missing from their pedestals

The garden has grown apart from the gardener

The famous woods torn up by tempest

I am no longer that tempest

I will no longer look up and see the absence of trees

This is not a descent into catacombs, an inevitable combustion, a darkening into blindness

Rather it is an approach on knees towards true sight

Departure

My last evening spent wandering along the docks.
By the foot-path, great iron rings.

Here is where the boats moor when the water rises.

The clouds gather themselves tightly together
as dervishes do after a period of whirling.

This should be a black and white film,
where I am the only one left,

sitting in front of the café,
waiting for the rain.

Briefly the sun pierces the clouds,
casts eerie shadows.

The water glows white.
My little cup glows white.

Letters in my bag for mailing.
Starlings clamber on the depot roof.

The sun dips into late afternoon.
For ten years I could not see.

Two boys are stacking rocks on top of one another.
I close my eyes and listen to the falling.

What about yesterday and the day before that?
Carry what you can in your hands. Scatter the rest.

The Year of Summer

You came down from the mountains to the shore with your father's voice ringing in your ears, saying over and over again the call to prayer.

The stairs leading down to the water are cracked and marked by awakening.

Awakening in the south the morning sun shines lemon yellow for eleven months, the leaves of the trees telling a book of eleven dreams.

In this book, the sky is sometimes lavender. In this book are colors you have never seen before.

In this book is the taste of white peach.

The blue-black sea turns milky under the noon-sun.

In the twelfth dream your father whispers your name into each of your folded ears.

In the year of summer you came south into a city of yellow and white, and what was told of this city was told in trees, and then in leaves, and then in light.

Journey

The wind over open water: sharp howling.

Guitar strings breaking.

Solstice having passed days longer now.

Beach aria.

Synaptic dysfunction or syntactic exuberance.

A small figure on the deck looking out across the blue-black.

The years since then drunk and unforgiving.

Wild roses crawl through the rough plank balcony.

Drinking bitter coffee on the terrace.

Weeks after that, alone in the vast public square.

Watching the crowds board the night boat back to the mainland.

Years later another journey you won't take.

Where will you now journey.

For a day.

Sounds of water.

You will sometime soon say: *I am coming home now.*

And not mean it.

What in your life have you meant.

A little inn perched in the hills above Calvi.

The cloud-sheathed cold.

Cold falling into the steep streets of the city.

You are still there.

Tissue-clouded moon swells above the blue-black.

A terse, obscene, spattering of stars.

A blue stone, fastened with a leather strap, cold against your chest.

Closing your eyes at the beach, listening to the rocks being piled, softly clacking against one another.

Another music for you.

Will you fall?

The wind presses against the portholes.

They rattle slightly in the night.

Rolling sound of rain pouring into the sea.

Wreaking the sound against sleep.

Waking with the light, the drunken year sinking.

3

Rain

With thick strokes of ink the sky fills with rain.
Pretending to run for cover but secretly praying for more rain.

Over the echo of the water, I hear a voice saying my name.
No one in the city moves under the quick sightless rain.

The pages of my notebook soak, then curl. I've written:
"Yogis opened their mouths for hours to drink the rain."

The sky is a bowl of dark water, rinsing your face.
The window trembles; liquid glass could shatter into rain.

I am a dark bowl, waiting to be filled.
If I open my mouth now, I could drown in the rain.

I hurry home as though someone is there waiting for me.
The night collapses into your skin. I am the rain.

The City

First the smell of wet earth.

Then fresh bread baking.

Great stone lions.
An obelisk.

An abandoned umbrella, broken by wind.

Each leaf on the drying pavement perfectly circled in rain.

This is where kings lie down.

This is where the wounded come to.

Event

Eight white birds, wings tipped with black, flying away. Snow stretches below from dark to darkness.

This is the image of the soul leaving, says Catherine. *I sent this postcard to my friends to announce the death of my sister.*

Dusty blue above the pyramid of Saqqara. The kingdom ends here and the desert begins.

Near a carved doorway, a guard lurks. For five pounds he lets me go down into the cold inner tombs.

There, the ancient etchings have been defaced by hieroglyphic graffiti. "First dynasty ruffians," the guard explains, in pieces.

The roof is missing from the temple at the gate. Only the pillars attest to it.

There is a consonant in the middle of my Arabic name that my tongue cannot manage.

I mispronounce myself.

In a room full of shards at the museum, realizing the Egyptian artists *practiced.* Over and over again: a human figure from the side. Two feet evenly placed.

No attempt at approaching or retreating figures.

I love this painting of the cathedral by Van Gogh, says Catherine. *There is no door, no way to get in.*

The River's Address

Slow in the evening light through tree-covered streets
sounds develop unenvelopable—

Troubadour, river-citizen, can you navigate the sound's course
to my far shore's ecstasy?

Be gray here, be broken and strafed, fully roused and drawn here,
like a compass needle, find yourself bound and unintelligible.

You followed the shrift north from the city into the mountains,
to the place you eddy, churn, spell out the moon's tidal courses.

River-chaser, compass-worn, here the source spills to the sea,
and here the waters wend from the sea back to the source.

Unsire yourself—instead of street-maps and sounding depths
trace your name, trace the trees, trace the night into your mind.

Close your eyes and listen to the sound—try to remember—
or try to forget—here is the place you could turn and return.

Precipice

We came to the next part together and eager,
trying on the accretion of coats,

your rough cheek against mine.
Cauldron eyes, you're striking, ferrous, uncurdling me.

All points of passage between two bodies
are points of danger.

What will be left as "what-I-believe-in"
hits the surface of the water from a great height?

Now no passengers, no sails, no anchor, only the me-craft,
swimming like crazy through fire-sleeved water with you.

Breathing it, being burned by it.
Thinking sometimes to walk on it.

Also being encircled.
Also being dispersed.

After I Said It

And after I said it
After I fell from the window

After I turned down the bed of history
Turned down the ocean road

Far enough down the ocean road
To dune-grasses, seagulls

In these other days
In another life

I did not say it
And in a different life

In my third life
I did not even think it

At the window
In my favorite blue shirt

Light sparkling up from the water
In my fourth life, angels

In my fifth life, windows

Ghost Boat

Sails quickly by the open window, a slight echo against a bottle
hung by the moon's sickly cords to mark its passage.

Sometimes I hear voices.

The settling house always creaks, marking time
invisibly, erratically.

I move about my business, unsettled.

There's a shivering echo under the second hand . . .

Erotic blasphemy of its unheard anchor,
dragging across the floorboards . . .

Thicket

The story unfolds like this: a blameless father
loves the as yet unharmed son.

The son is somewhat randy and alarmed
at his appearance in an orthodox world.

Does it hurt him that he's been cut from the tribe of sons
who believe, are unarmed, who recite all the rules?

It's the father who believes in God.
The son believes in the father.

The father in this story is guileless,
not trying to call God's bluff.

And unbelievably to all,
the son willingly opens his throat to the universe.

Neither one of them seeking to see Him,
not saying His name, not asking to be saved.

Hunger

In the Christian version of the story,
Ishmael lies limp on the ground,

Hagar, mother of the hungry, beginning to rise up,
one arm flailing, stricken.

She does not even see the necessary angel,
coming to reveal the hidden spring's location.

Unlearn the passage of time.

Unlearn the snatches of music.

The wind which followed you to this place.

In the Muslim version, she knows Ishmael is dying,
but doesn't wait to find out what happens next.

Like Abraham with the sacrificial knife in his hand,
she does not expect rescue from the sky.

She would never expect the earth beneath the boy would crack,
a spring would bubble up there, water filling his mouth.

Alone in the desert, between two mountains, she's gone
before his heels begin hammering the rock in the spasm of death—

The Return of Music

The bridge of birches stretches down to the horizon.
A ridge of wings descending into the leaves.

Turn now in a note sent thither.
Thither around and the wind strikes.

Orange, the trees are aflame.
Scarlet. Called here, you came.

Light carving shadows into tree bark.
You translate this into other languages, all antiquated and still.

An anthem of ether. Shorn, you always wondered:
what willful course have you carved through your history?

In the tree-capped valley, the lustrous wind chafes through.
Leaf fence uncurl. The valley wends the way the music went.

The sapphire sky, unbelievable, but there.
These moments against the years you cannot believe.

This hover of music winging down from the mountains
you cannot believe.

But here in the trees, here above the river, here as the season
stitches itself into fog then frost, you will.

Here as you unfold, unsummon, uncry, you will.

Unopened, you will. Unhappen, you will.

These moments against the years, you will.

Unmoment you will.

Unyear you will. Unyou you will.

Unwill you will—

4

Dear Rumi

You've forgotten the other life in which
Shams-e-Tabriz threw your books into the fountain.

The ink, finally unrecognizable,
reached for you with dissipating lust.

Once I went up the mountain at daybreak, and still met pilgrims
coming down who had woken for the journey earlier.

In the tomb of not-Shams I prayed and prayed to be found.
Am I the sun inside me?

Shams will walk out the back door and never return.
You will go mad—spend years looking for him.

One day in the marketplace, estranged and weeping,
you will understand the farthest mosque is the one within,

and that the sun in the sky is not the one you orbit around,
nor the one who went out the back door and never returned.

Somewhere in the world now, every minute,
a sun is dropping over the horizon into yesterday.

At the fountain in the village square,
the books are still sinking, bereft of your hands.

Even the mountains are bending down to try to save them.
Dear Shams-e-Tabriz, I do not mourn.

You spindle me, sun-thorn, to the sky.

Said: In the Rain

Wide in the hills he came to unearth the golden tablets.
You put all this together one afternoon walking home in rain.

Last night, after playing Satie you briefly believed
the back of the mind was the only religion that mattered.

Perturbed, you never wanted words graven in fire,
but wished to be found there, buried in the hill-dirt,

in the rain, a follower of a religion of water,
and why not?

Why not be an acolyte of the twisting ribbon of river?
What else floods its way from great rock to oblivion?

In a night divided into Satie and self-evidence,
why not the religion of what always seeps back to itself?

Why not a religion of water in a time of great fires?
You fear you may drown, but your birth in it implies otherwise.

Not that it is impossible to drown, but that
this whole time you have been drowning.

Maya or Mayaar

You will always be gone.
All matter edges itself to dust.

Sunlight a pool or flower or fountain.
Music breaking the room to shards.

But why fret? In one language *maya* means
"all these molecules are breaking."

Your hands, the music, the paper, are not real.
Not pieces of liquid or light, but light years.

On the other side of the world you were taught
other names for things.

Mr. William touches the surface of the water with his hand,
says: *mayaar.*

Water, light, light on the surface of the water
or shining from beneath the water, are all fibs and fortunes.

Music can break its fall.
Light could speak.

A year could open between *maya* and *mayaar*
That would provide perfect pitch against which you could practice.

Beyond that you're flailing, moon-licked, stunned,
Music, sunstruck, rainstorm, begun—

Rhyme

Restless your surface rise up be unraveled
Unwrap the dusk to a light shell

All the crevices in the oak are pierced by moon chords
Rough sky unlocked shredded by meteors

Vision-dusted thirsty night's blue fastenings
Second time this earth year the sun I leapt up in anger

Birch bark unribbons to reveal all the secret roads
Sun soaks the day's façade in clouds and clots

How fully I tack myself to the wind of anger
While you life up the mountain match-struck immaculate

Sun oracle prophesy solar flares along my skin
Wind oracle forgive me perennially rude

A long secret road unfastens from earth
Frozen luck-thin snapping in unseasonable cold

Four white roads crossing nothing into nothing
Such low light through the bottle hanging

Breath sieve mountain come break at the sea
When lava that new country first enters the water

The rock an immense fire river pouring onto the beach
Saying all the words in the world rhyme

Will wind winterful wending flood
A bell brooding somewhere oracle

A wolf-note sounding against the hush
Somewhere thorned to the sun-spindle

Spendthrift wind run spindle din drift
Music kin shift cindered candle theft

Soot riddle wicked fire
Ash answer wind mouth

Cave earth throat explain
Why all the unhinged worlds rhyme

Olga omen old friend
Meddle metal birth foam

Green notebook winter road
Over sound world sheet

Ocean home metal written sun verse
Curt whisper absurd wishes winter thirst

Sleep Bowl

The light bowl
of your voice

Sounds across the surface of my sleep
bit by bit coming to it

White wings brushing
against the eardrum

You were named in me thirteen years ago
by my mother rust-clad at the promise river

The dozen different versions of me
being carried on drafts away

Sleep little sweat-lodge, spirit house,
imaginary boy, petaled to my side, breathing

Saying his father's name
across the bowl of my sleep

Glacier

The wind tells all the dream-lives:
in one, walking alone in a cactus garden.

Or there's another: me, old, dying, in a wind-filled beach-house.

Polished hardwood floors, the kitchen full of relatives and friends
who have come to be with me at the end.

We sometimes find ourselves on the widow's walk watching the water,
reminiscing about a life that hasn't happened.

Cactus garden, you are a ruse.

Beach-house you are only an echo.

My seventy-third year is a glacier,
advancing across me in my sleep,

decanting my dream-lives,
sculpting new topography as it recedes . . .

The Book

Before I came into the air from my mother,
I breathed her water.

Below any temple steps, there is always a beggar
who having renounced the world, seeks forms of direction.

Blind sometimes, or in ecstasy,
the book has become not a book.

Sometimes I wake up starving.
It is hard to know when to eat.

The page, square cover, sewn edge, table edge,
my weak sense of direction, collapsing to smoke.

When I wake like this, when neither the dream nor the day
have ruptured themselves into belief, the book unbuckles

and I think all of life is by faith only, that we are never delivered
from original water, that we are all a single equation

that approaches the axis, never arrives.

The New World

Ask your brother why he will not come to you.
The moon has fallen, spilt from your skin,

and all the broad fields are crying
we are done.

The lion-flowers flare once to tell you we've been here before,
we know the end: your hand, the long road in your hand,

the forked tongue in your hand.
Your brother is coming to speak in tongues.

Saying: *let the molten mortar of the fallen walls cool.*
Let the temper of the men cool.

We've burned out the rainforge, collapsed all the predicting tables.
The sky has turned into a blue stone, rising out of the sea.

Imagine the geographic possibility:
your brother, again in the trenches.

Still, there are other chances: sculptor, sculpt it back to rock.
Thrash the bread of this back to bran.

Return the lost dove to its sea-faring perch.
Now, dove, re-seed the burned fields, travail the sated,

and guide us to the new world, quite lonesome, quite far,
but agreeable, and green.

Danger

The sky-wheel spins and a voice unravels

Now you will need to weave without thread

Now you will no longer hear

Yesterday a voice talking with me slowly, quietly

A silver thread going from her mouth

Into my ear

Lying in bed this morning giving everything up

The years

The years

Well

The brook flowing slowly
Endlessly rowing through impassable dark

Urged on by a rattlesnake soundtrack
Plain blue, solo, artless

I am kept unto prayer
Returned again to unbelief

And when she was sent to me
The well

I sang *thou art my sister, my broad year,*
My seed-ear, my leaf . . .

July

We lay down in the graveyard, hinged there.

Emerald moss growing thickly in the chiseled letters.

You're explaining how trees actually breathe.

Green in the names and trees went up to join gray in the sky.

Then the gray-green sky came down in breaths to my lips and
sipped me.

NOTES

Gallery: "The Man Who Taught William Blake Painting in His Dreams" is a painting by William Blake.

Renunciation: The epigraph is from Dickinson's third letter to Higginson.

Travel: The italicized quote is a slight adaptation of George Braque, from *Painters on Painting,* edited by Eric Protter, Dover Editions.

In the Agnes Martin Room: The Agnes Martin Room is at Dia:Beacon Riggio Galleries in Beacon, NY.

Night Boat: Mister Stevarius is online: www.stevarius.com

Cemetery at Montparnasse: The epitaph is carved into the headstone of sculptor Leopold Kretz.

Event: The first painting described is "Seagulls in Flight" by Nicolas de Stael. The second is "L'église d'Auvers-sur-Oise" by Van Gogh. This poem is for Catherine Aga.

Dear Rumi: Shams-e-Tabriz's name means "Sun." The "a" in "Shams" is pronounced like the "a" in "ago."

Rhyme: "All the words in the world rhyme" is rumored to have been said by Olga Broumas at a seminar at Sarah Lawrence College. "Green Notebook, Winter Road" is the title of a book by Jane Cooper.

Gloryland, Anne Marie Macari
Polar, Dobby Gibson
Pennyweight Windows: New & Selected Poems, Donald Revell
Matadora, Sarah Gambito
In the Ghost-House Acquainted, Kevin Goodan
The Devotion Field, Claudia Keelan
Into Perfect Spheres Such Holes Are Pierced, Catherine Barnett
Goest, Cole Swensen
Night of a Thousand Blossoms, Frank X. Gaspar
Mister Goodbye Easter Island, Jon Woodward
The Devil's Garden, Adrian Matejka
The Wind, Master Cherry, the Wind, Larissa Szporluk
North True South Bright, Dan Beachy-Quick
My Mojave, Donald Revell
Granted, Mary Szybist
Sails the Wind Left Behind, Alessandra Lynch
Sea Gate, Jocelyn Emerson
An Ordinary Day, Xue Di
The Captain Lands in Paradise, Sarah Manguso
Ladder Music, Ellen Doré Watson
Self and Simulacra, Liz Waldner
Live Feed, Tom Thompson
The Chime, Cort Day
Utopic, Claudia Keelan
Pity the Bathtub Its Forced Embrace of the Human Form, Matthea Harvey
Isthmus, Alice Jones
The Arrival of the Future, B.H. Fairchild
The Kingdom of the Subjunctive, Suzanne Wise
Camera Lyrica, Amy Newman
How I Got Lost So Close to Home, Amy Dryansky
Zero Gravity, Eric Gamalinda
Fire & Flower, Laura Kasischke
The Groundnote, Janet Kaplan
An Ark of Sorts, Celia Gilbert
The Way Out, Lisa Sewell
The Art of the Lathe, B.H. Fairchild

Alice James Books has been publishing exclusively poetry since 1973. One of the few presses in the country that is run collectively, the cooperative selects manuscripts for publication through both regional and national annual competitions. New regional authors become active members of the cooperative, participating in the editorial decisions of the press. The press, which historically has placed an emphasis on publishing women poets, was named for Alice James, sister of William and Henry, whose fine journal and gift for writing went unrecognized within her lifetime.

TYPESET AND DESIGNED BY MIKE BURTON

PRINTED BY THOMSON-SHORE